Animal Feeding Time

FIRST EDITION
Project Editor Deborah Murrell; **Art Editor** Catherine Goldsmith; **Senior Art Editor** Clare Shedden;
Managing Editor Bridget Gibbs; **US Editor** Regina Kahney; **Senior DTP Designer** Bridget Roseberry;
Production Shivani Pandey; **Picture Librarian** Diane Legrande; **Picture Researcher** Marie Osborn;
Jacket Designer Karen Burgess; **Natural History Consultant** Theresa Greenaway;
Reading Consultant Linda Gambrell, PhD

THIS EDITION
Editorial Management by Oriel Square
Produced for DK by WonderLab Group LLC
Jennifer Emmett, Erica Green, Kate Hale, *Founders*

Editors Grace Hill Smith, Libby Romero, Michaela Weglinski;
Photography Editors Kelley Miller, Annette Kiesow, Nicole DiMella;
Managing Editor Rachel Houghton; **Designers** Project Design Company;
Researcher Michelle Harris; **Copy Editor** Lori Merritt; **Indexer** Connie Binder;
Proofreader Larry Shea; **Reading Specialist** Dr. Jennifer Albro; **Curriculum Specialist** Elaine Larson

Published in the United States by DK Publishing
1745 Broadway, 20th Floor, New York, NY 10019

Copyright © 2023 Dorling Kindersley Limited
DK, a Division of Penguin Random House LLC
23 24 25 26 27 10 9 8 7 6 5 4 3 2 1
001–333431–Apr/2023

A catalog record for this book
is available from the Library of Congress.
HC ISBN: 978-0-7440-6693-7
PB ISBN: 978-0-7440-6694-4

DK books are available at special discounts when purchased
in bulk for sales promotions, premiums, fundraising, or
educational use. For details, contact: DK Publishing Special Markets,
1745 Broadway, 20th Floor, New York, NY 10019
SpecialSales@dk.com

Printed and bound in China

The publisher would like to thank the following for their kind permission to reproduce their images:
a=above; c=center; b=below; l=left; r=right; t=top; b/g=background

Getty Images: Grant Thomas / iStock 8-9; Moment / Moelyn Photos 28-29; **Dreamstime.com:** Jezbennett 14-15;
Shutterstock.com: Binturong-tonoscarpe 32br, diegooscar01 25t, Daniel Guertin 4-5, Katesalin Heinio 24,
Rudi Hulshof 21cr, 30bl, marseus 3, Nicola_K_photos 6-7, Marcin Osman 12-13, Stu Porter 26-27, Dr Morley Read 22-23bc,
30clb (termites), Simply Photos 19, Silvia Truessel 10-11, Oleksandr Umanskyi 16-17

Cover images: *Front:* **123RF.com:** Duncan Noakes l; **Dreamstime.com:** Anastasiya Aheyeva b, Colorfuelstudio crb;
Back: **Alamy Stock Photo:** Elvele Images Ltd cla; **Dreamstime.com:** Dragoneye cra, Roomyana ca
All other images © Dorling Kindersley

For the curious
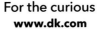

Animal Feeding Time

Lee Davis

DK

Contents

Morning Meal

It is morning.
The sun is rising.
Animals that eat
in the daytime
start to look for food.

A gorilla yawns in his nest.
He reaches out his
hairy hand to feel
for a tasty plant.
He has breakfast in bed.

A herd of elephants is ready for breakfast, too. The elephants wrap their trunks around clumps of grass.

They curl their trunks
to break off the grass
and put it in their mouths.

Another elephant snaps off branches from a big tree. He chews the bark on each branch.

bark

A large elephant
knows there are
some crunchy
seedpods in
the tall trees.
He stretches his
trunk to reach them.

seedpods

Late Lunch

Zebras reach down to nibble the grass.

They bite the grass
with their front teeth.

A giraffe can reach
the treetops
with her long neck.
She wraps her tongue
around the tasty,
tender shoots.
Her tongue tears
the shoots
off the branches.

shoots ———

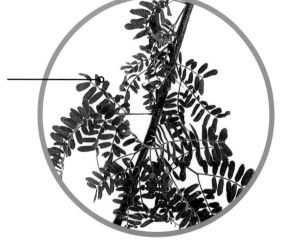

A rhino spends most
of the day eating grass.
An oxpecker clings
to the rhino.

oxpecker

The oxpecker eats
ticks and insects
on the rhino's skin.
He pecks at them
with his pointed beak.

tick

A chimpanzee is looking for termites to eat.
He digs with a stick into a huge termite hill.
He makes a large hole in the termite hill, and the termites spill out.

termites

A herd of buffalo
moves to the
river for a drink.
Crocodiles
watch and wait.
They are as
still as rocks.

Slowly, a crocodile
swims closer.
Can he grab
a young buffalo
for his dinner?

Evening Snack

Hippos spend the hot day
in the water.
In the evening,
the air is cooler.

So, they come out
to eat the short grass
on the river banks.

As the sun sets,
the elephants enjoy
a late evening snack.

They eat more fruit and then have a long, cool drink.

Glossary

bark
the outer part of a tree trunk or branches

seedpod
a case with the seeds of a plant inside

shoot
young plants that grow from larger ones

termites
insects that feed on wood and build mound

tick
a bug on the skin of an animal that sucks its blood

Index

Quiz

Answer the questions to see what you have learned. Check your answers with an adult.

1. What does the gorilla like to eat from its nest?

2. How does the giraffe eat shoots from tree branches?

3. Why does the oxpecker cling to the rhino's back?

4. How does the chimpanzee eat termites?

5. Which animal from this book is your favorite? What does it like to eat?

1. Plants 2. It tears them off the branches with its tongue 3. To eat ticks on the rhino's skin
4. He digs a hole in the termite hill using a stick
5. Answers will vary